How To Help Someone Who Is

Grieving

R. Diane Ashley, M.P.C.

DEDICATION

This book is dedicated to my son Nic Ashley. He became an amazing man who any mother would be proud to say is hers. His influence on others and his love of helping emotionally lost teenagers will never be forgotten.

Appreciation

I would like to thank my husband, Ron, our younger son, Josh, who still lived at home during the writing of this book, and my sister Billie, for their patience and support while I wrote. Their encouragement and confidence in me were invaluable.

CONTENTS

A kind gesture can reach a wound
that only compassion can heal

Steve Maraboli

INTRODUCTION

Although I started life in the home of my parents, I was removed to my grandmother's house when I was ten. Between these two locations, I suffered many years of physical and emotional abuse and sexual assault. In addition, during my early adult life, I went through a difficult period caused by a misdiagnosed medical condition. These were difficult things for me to deal with. However, nothing I had experienced in my life compared to the debilitating pain I endured as a result of our son's death.

Several people tried to help my husband and I after this happened. In spite of all their efforts though, it seemed like the only individuals able to understand what we needed were those who had already gone through a nightmare like ours. Unfortunately for them, assisting us meant they had to relive a lot of their own traumas.

Since that time, a lot of people have asked me how to help others who are suffering as my husband and I had suffered. Sadly, there are no easy answers. Because grief is highly personal and specific to each situation and each person, creating a definitive handbook of how to comfort someone who hurts is not possible. However, there are some things you can do that might give a mourner respite from pain without making him or her worse. Identifying these is the purpose of this book.

Although I've dedicated the bulk of this writing to helping someone who is mourning, I have included a brief overview of my life at the end of this book for those interested in reading it. I chose to incorporate it, because I felt it offered readers a chance to see that I am not just sharing educational knowledge about trauma. I have lived through it.

A section of this writing also addresses the grieving process and some of the serious mental health issues it can create. Grief left unresolved can cause a plethora of issues. If untreated, several can deteriorate into serious emotional conditions. Having experienced some of them myself after our son's death, I understand how debilitating they can be. Consequently, to help you help someone you care about, I have included them in this book.

Although this book is beneficial for individuals, I encourage you to also read it as part of a study or support group. Doing this provides several benefits that you might gain beyond just reading alone. It may help you better remember what you have read, provide you a resource in learning what may or may not have worked for others, and enable you to share some of your own experiences as well.

I would also like to encourage you respect the culture of the people you are trying to help. They will probably have different values, heritages, spiritual beliefs, unique ways of coping with their hurt, or in the case of death, rituals they observe to honor the deceased and process their own pain. These may be foreign to you, but to the hurting, they play a vital role in the healing process.

It is my sincerest hope that those who read this book will find something in it to help others. To that end, I encourage you to not just read a couple of chapters but all of it. Sometimes something that appears to be innocuous can hurt the worst. Reading this book through may help you identify those things before you make the mistake of doing them to someone else.

Section One

HOW TO HELP

Chapter 1

WHAT GRIEF LOOKS LIKE

Perhaps the best image to describe grief is its similarity to an ocean wave. When stormy weather begins, the water becomes turbulent, creating crashing waves that build in intensity. As the water moves toward land, it appears to grow in ferocity. After the wave peaks its intensity weakens. Once it crashes against the shoreline, its last strength ebbs, and the water recedes into the ocean to wait until the next wave to starts growing.

The storm represents the trauma. When it first hits, mourners will most likely feel emotional upheaval, turbulence, and chaos. With this, they experience "grief waves" that strike one almost on top of the next. Mourners might appear calm one moment and then suddenly escalate toward an explosive condition in the next, because, as grief wells up inside it grows until it becomes nearly impossible to contain. When grievers reach a breaking point, they might experience a severely crushing moment. Emotions may become erratic, and they might display abnormal behaviors like panic attacks, gut—wrenching, uncontrollable sobbing, or even anger.

Once the intensity of the pain decreases, grievers will most likely feel as though their strength has ebbed;—similar to the ocean wave losing its energy. After the final vestiges of hurt have subsided, they will probably feel drained. The respite this produces only lasts until the next grief wave starts building. The greater the level of trauma—death, unwanted divorce, and so on—the more often grief waves hit; the weaker the storm the less frequent the waves.

At the onset of grief, this cycle will repeat itself often. This can make the griever appear as though he or she is in a constant state of flux between calm and chaos. However, as time moves forward, grief waves should get farther apart. The time it takes for this to occur is generally dependent upon the nature of the trauma and the unique life shape of the person suffering. Some people may process their pain relatively quickly; others may take years to work through it. As is the case with parental bereavement, though, the pain could last a lifetime. The worst of the pain should heal with time but some intensity of it may continue for the duration of a person's life (Lichtenthal, Currier, Neimeyer, and Keesee 2010).

The grieving process is not only wearying for people who are experiencing it but also for the people trying to help grievers. This is because the violent rawness of pain increases with significant loss and radiates outward, affecting anyone in proximity to it. Succinctly put, hurting people emit waves of pain that bounce against anyone who happens to be in their general vicinity.

It's like when someone throws a rubber ball. It moves outward from the person who throws it, bouncing against whomever it comes in contact with. Similarly, pain radiates off the person experiencing it and touches anyone in the vicinity. Those who feel it usually become uncomfortable and start looking for a way to make the feeling stop. Thus, there may be a temptation to try to push a griever to "hurry up and get over it".

If you feel as if you are in this category, you need to remember that the grief–wave–cycle is not about you. It is about the ones who are mourning, and it is their outlet for maintaining sanity so that pain does not consume them. Regardless of how uncomfortable or drained you might feel when near someone in the grip of a wave, resist the natural urge to force him or her in the direction of moving on. Make room for the person to both express and expel grief, or the individual might not find healthy healing.

A person's cognitive processing abilities and emotional condition develop as a result of life experiences (see section II of this book, "Factors That Affect Grief Processing"). Although there are commonalities in the grieving process, each person is still going to travel through it in his or her own way and at his or her own pace.

Chapter 2

IT'S NOT ABOUT YOU

W e have no idea how much trauma can be added to grievers when we make their pain about us. Although it is inconceivable that anyone would do this deliberately, it happens all the time. We just don't realize it. People are generally more likely to react instead of thinking things through, so they frequently don't take time to identify their motivations for doing or saying what they do.

It is natural human tendency to want to help someone who is hurting. However, most of us act on the need to help because it makes *us* feel better. Then, because we feel better, we make the assumption that the mourner also feels better. The thought that a person might actually feel worse because of what we have said or done never crosses our minds. Instead, we just expect that our good intentions made a positive contribution. Our intent is not malicious and there are some cases where helping might bring a griever relief; but most of those suffering would probably agree that it doesn't. Even knowing this, when we see someone experiencing deep pain, we still tend to give in to the compulsion to do something. Struggling with the pain that unexpectedly hits us, we surrender to the pressure of wanting to make it stop.

What does this look like? Often, especially at the onset of the trauma, it involves touching, unsolicited hugs, patting a knee, or putting an arm around a shoulder are common examples. It might also include behaviors such as forced prayer, unwanted conversation, or tiresome visits. Succinctly, it is doing things *we* believe will make the mourner better, while not giving consideration to how our actions are actually affecting him or her. When we act on our feelings rather than finding out what the hurting person needs, we make the situation about us, not the griever.

Dealing with grief is hard for anyone to do. But we should never force a mourner to choose between accepting our brand of comfort, and hurting our feelings.

I once attended a training seminar wherein numerous speakers had been invited. Among them were hospice representatives. During their segment, a spokeswoman for the organization discussed the nature of grief and included some dos and don'ts for helping. Their session was open floor, meaning that individuals were allowed to ask questions or interject pertinent, brief comments. I have lived on both sides of the discussion as both a mourner and a comforter. Consequently, I connected with much of what was being said. The dialogue eventually veered away from a discussion about the emotions felt before an imminent death to emotions felt after death occurs. The seminar was open floor so I decided to share some of what had happened to us.

After our son died, it seemed as if everyone wanted to touch us. At first, I tolerated as much as I could, because I didn't want to hurt anyone's feelings or be rude. As wave upon wave of people kept coming to offer their comfort, though, I finally got to the place where I could barely stand physical contact. People weren't purposely trying to cause us discomfort. Their intentions were to help. However, after literally hundreds of people had touched us—some numerous times, our skin became highly sensitive and sore. I did appreciate those who came but I began to dread having to make physical contact with each new person who approached.

My husband began successfully putting out "keep off" signals by not getting out of his chair to greet newcomers when they arrived. I often just avoided them. Unfortunately, this didn't always work. Not realizing I just needed to be left alone, comforters would track me down if they did not see me.

Finally, I reached a breaking point, which forced me to make a tough choice: be rude by telling people to stop touching me, or be kind by letting them push me to the brink of insanity. It was a hard decision to make, but I was suffering severe grief. And adding physical pain to an already traumatized mind was more than I could take. So, even though I knew people were just trying to offer what they felt was comfort, I made them stop touching me. No more hugs, brief pats on the back, kisses on the top of my head, holding my hand to pray, putting an arm around my shoulders, or sitting right next to me. No more touching.

The responses I received were somewhat surprising. Shock registered on some faces, as though I were committing a crime against them. One woman even yelled at me saying that she just wanted to help me, but I wouldn't let her. All of these people were more concerned about their need to give solace than they were about what I actually needed. Some people seemed to understand though. It was these people that gave the most comfort.

After I shared all this with the audience, a woman in the group spoke up, vehemently disagreeing with me. She stated that giving someone a hug was important, as it let the hurting person know she cared. I asked if she had ever lost anyone close to her. She looked slightly militant and said she hadn't, but that didn't mean she couldn't give comfort to someone grieving. She said her desire to give a hug showed mourners how much she cared and supported them.

One of the hospice officials interrupted the woman and stated what I had been thinking. The representative told the woman that her insistence on giving a hug put her in the position of making the mourner's situation about herself and her need to give comfort, not about what the hurting person actually needed.

If we really care about grieving people, we should want to help them based on what *they* need rather than what *we* feel. We should make the effort to identify what we can do for them and not force hugs or some other type of unsolicited action on them because it makes us feel better. If we don't want to increase their suffering, then we need to control our feelings in favor of respecting their pain. It's not that a hug, a touch, or a prayer is inappropriate. But it's best to ask before you initiate action. If we do not want to make their pain about us, then we need to be certain that they aren't saying yes because they don't want to offend us; they are saying yes because they really do need human contact in that moment.

Chapter 3

THE VISIT

Oddly enough, most of us assume that mourners understand we are there because we care. After all, most people would not visit the home of grieving persons without a purpose in mind. But what is that purpose? Are we going because we genuinely care about them and the loss they have suffered, or is there some other reason we feel compelled to go? Are we attending for personal reasons, or do we genuinely want to help? Our automatic response will usually be because we want to help. However, if we don't carefully examine our motivations for attending a mourner, our presence may actually cause more harm than good.

Although we might cite numerous reasons for going, here are three of the more common. After a careful analysis of your motivating factors, which would you fall into?

- *Those who are obligated*: Some individuals feel compelled to go. They visit grievers simply to assuage their conscience, by doing their duty. They believe they have a responsibility to the mourner that obliges them to go and make a "required" appearance. Once that's done, they feel they have discharged their duty, and they leave feeling good about themselves for the contribution they made toward giving solace. In their minds, attendance equals support, and without having to say it, the griever is expected to know this. Yet, aside from showing up to make their selves feel good; these individuals have done nothing that could really be defined as comfort.

- *Those with personal connections*: Some individuals have personal connections with mourners that create a deep–seated honest need to do what they can when called upon. Their relationship is such that they will carry on through the trauma, regardless of how long it takes or how difficult it may sometimes be. They are in it for the long–haul, and they will stick it out with their friend until the individual can once again stand on his or her own.

- *Those with a genuine desire to help*: Some may be there just because they care. These people may not know the griever well, but they want to help. They might be humanitarians who care about other human beings, individuals who have experienced some- thing similar, or maybe some of both. They might even be people who have never met the griever, but having experienced something similar their selves, like the death of a child for instance, they want to help. Regardless of why, these people are all driven by the same thing: an honest desire to support, in whatever way they can, someone who is hurting.

I was once at the home of a family who was suffering due to a member's death, where I observed a group of friends. Each woman paid her respects to the family when she arrived, and then gravitated to where the others had assembled to socialize and catch up. They stayed for a while, occasionally becoming loud. Watching these women, it was apparent their conduct was not purposely cruel. They were just so engaged in their socializing that they seemed to have forgotten where they were, and why they were there. Their opportunity catch up had occurred because they were in the home of someone suffering the loss of a loved one.

Another example of this was the dinner after our son's funeral. He was twenty-two and married when he died. His wife asked to have his wake at our house. She didn't feel that the church was nice enough, so wanted to do it elsewhere. He is our son, so we would have agreed to anything. She said that her family just wanted to use the backyard and deck area because it was warm outside, and the inside of our home was too small. None of her family offered to help; neither did they show up the day before the dinner to help with preparations. Instead, my husband and younger son who were also grieving, put up tables, setup tented canopies for food, and arranged shaded areas for people to sit and eat.

After the funeral, a few of the women from my daughter-in-law's family arrived and started moving things inside. They told me that, even though it was late afternoon, it was too hot outside, so everything was coming inside. They never asked me; nor were they kind about it. They just told me what was going to happen. I said no, reminding them that the house was not big enough. One of the women firmly told me that it didn't matter. She then glared at me as though daring me to disagree. I did, telling her no once again. I felt violated. We had just buried our baby, and these women didn't have enough decency to respect that. Instead, they tried to bully me into agreeing to what they wanted. After they pushed me the third time, I became angry and told them to get the stuff out of my house. In the end, it didn't matter. Once everyone had left, I found food ground into the rugs, drinks spilled everywhere, and dirty dishes and garbage piled up. They did what they wanted to do, in spite of the cost to my husband and me, leaving a huge mess for us to clean after they had gone. My husband and I were already in an emotionally and physically drained condition. The callousness of those women made me feel completely abused and broken.

On that day, it was not the hundred or more people who attended the wake who helped and comforted us. Instead, it was my baby sister, a sister-in-law, and a few others who stayed after most people had left. Although they couldn't do much about the damage to the floors, they did their best to clean up most of the mess everyone else had left behind.

In most cases, our mere presence is not what brings peace to someone dealing with grief–but what we do. Giving support means finding ways to help ease someone's burden rather than increase it. A good way to do this is to first identify what our plans are *before* we connect with the grievers. Contact someone who knows them and find out ahead of time what you can do that will help. If that isn't possible, then consider taking a card with money in it. You would be surprised at how even twenty dollars during times of trauma can make a difference.

Even though culture is mentioned in a couple of other places in this book, due to its importance in relation to a visit, I am discussing it here as well. Respect the culture of the people you are trying to help. To you, their practices, values, and beliefs may be foreign, but to the hurting, they can play a vital role in the healing process.

If grievers want to talk, or they ask you to stay, try not to stay overly long. While you are there, try not to ask for anything if you can help it—not even a drink. The last thing already—drained people need is to wait on someone. Consider making this standard practice, unless you are asked to do otherwise by the griever. An example of this might be if you are requested to participate in a family ritual honoring someone who has died.

If its clear medical assistance may be needed, get help. Go for the purpose of genuinely helping those who hurt. Don't make them worse.

Chapter 4

GRIEF IS NOT AN AGENDA

It is hard to imagine anyone would have the audacity to use another's pain as a means to promote a strongly held belief, yet it happens all the time. How? When, instead of giving real comfort, we use the traumatic situation as an opportunity to further our agendas.

Politicians play on the vulnerable emotions of those either suffering or affected by someone else's pain; their purpose, of course, is to advance campaigns or gain support for promoted platforms. Leaders across the globe, including terrorists, embrace the technique as well, using it to secure blind loyalty. Even general laypeople and family members have used someone's pain as a means of furthering personal agendas. Consider interfamilial manipulation and an individual's purpose for doing it.

A woman once shared with me the story of her brother's death. Because of childhood abuse, he had struggled with clinical depression for most of his life. After many years of living in a roller-coaster condition, he was tired and decided to just give up—he committed suicide. The woman had been very close to her brother and the pain she suffered with the loss of their relationship was devastating.

After his funeral, she was discussing her brother's death with a woman who had experienced a similar loss. The woman told the grieving sister that she knew her own brother had a chance to go to heaven. She let the sister know that it was too bad her brother had gone to hell. This self-righteous woman's need to promote her personal suicide = hell agenda was more important to her than any concern she might have felt over causing additional suffering. It did not matter to her that the young man had suffered with depression for years, nor did she even consider that just maybe he had been damaged as a child through no fault of his own. All that mattered was her need to feel as though she had done her religious duty.

Although the above story supports the damage caused by promoting platforms, perhaps two of the most well—known examples are 9/11 and Sandy Hook Elementary School. Both events have had the unfortunate effect of creating an endless sympathy pool from which politicians, organizations, and others in need of agenda support draw from.

We might find it hard to believe anyone would willingly use grief and loss for personal gain, but there is no denying it occurs. People with similar personal stories might feel entitled to use others' tragedies in support of their goals. However, that does not mean they have a right to inflict their beliefs on those suffering. Grievers have already been traumatized enough by what has happened to them. Consider their situation and have mercy on them. Leave the agenda at home and just focus on giving comfort to the hurting person.

Chapter 5

PLEASE DON'T TOUCH ME

Although physical contact was discussed in chapter 2, its potential for increasing a griever's pain necessitates additional discussion. As stated earlier, touching can either help someone or make him or her worse. A hug or other type of physical contact generally makes the person initiates it to feel good. It allows them to feel as though they have done their part to offer comfort. However, we should never think that once we have made physical contact with hurting people, our duty to them has been discharged.

People need to have contact with others to feel better, but that doesn't mean they are looking for a hug from everyone they come in contact with. Real comfort—producing touches are generally accepted by mourners from the people they connect well with at that moment. Of course, we all like to believe we are in this group, but most of us probably aren't.

Membership in the "touching group" will most likely always be in flux. A few members will consistently be part of it throughout the mourning period, which can last months or even years. Others, though, will move out to make room for new individuals, as grievers' progress through each stage of their pain. This is because what grievers need to receive defines the identity of the group. As their needs change, so do the members of the group. For example, one moment a hurting person might want to be held by a close family member. In another, it could be a total stranger who has experienced something similar. It's oftentimes hard to watch someone else give the solace that we feel we should be offering to the person we care about. However, if our need to feel validated causes us to force something on the griever, we will most likely hurt, instead of help, the person we are so desperate to aid.

Watch a mourner's body language before you actually reach out and touch. Make sure the grieving person is not radiating keep–away signals including

- tensing of the shoulders when you lean toward him or her;

- flinching as you start to reach out to the person or at the beginning of the touch;

- a slight pulling away at first contact;

- leaning away from you as you lean in;

- fidgeting;

- leaving the room as you approach to avoid being touched.

An example that supports this idea is the story of a woman whose child had died. Moments after being told that the child had not survived, the mother was sitting in a slightly slumped but tensed-up position, in shock. Unprepared for the loss, she was trying to mentally navigate the surreal waves of devastation assaulting her. Seeing her in this condition, a man approached, put his hand on top of her head, and began praying. As he spoke, he started applying increasing amounts of pressure to her head. Being in shock, at first she didn't respond to what he was doing. However, as he began pushing her head toward her shoulders, the woman finally had enough. Standing, she forced the man's hand off and moved away. Although the man no doubt felt his actions were the best thing that could help the woman, she did not want the prayer, physical contact, or attention forced on her. The woman shared that the minister had made an already bad situation worse, leaving her to feel numb and bruised. She said she believed in God and his divine purpose, but at that moment, forced prayer was the last thing she wanted.

As stated earlier, there are times when people need physical contact. Receiving help from someone in this manner can soothe people, and for a few moments, it might even help alleviate the pain they feel. However, initiating touch is not the best way to assist. It might make us feel good, but it may not help the recipient.

Consider asking before you offer physical contact. Don't query, "May I give you a hug?" That is a statement about your need. Instead, try asking, "Would you like a hug, or would you rather not be touched right now?" This will give the individual an opportunity to choose. Remember, it could be that a quiet presence, or someone to draw strength from without physical touch, is what a hurting person may need most at that time.

Chapter 6

"WHAT HAPPENED?"

J ust about everyone has asked this question, because everyone wants to hear the story. At first, just an overview will suffice. Soon, though, people start asking the griever to repeat the story again—but with the details. After that, mourners are then subjected to rounds of questions, because the listeners want clarification of each story piece so they can better understand what occurred.

Even though the story is new to us, for the hurting person, it is something he or she is being asked to retell over and over again. Every answered phone call or each new face that arrives means the hurting person is going to have to tell the story again. Each retelling makes the griever relive the pain.

Sometimes a mourner may not mind sharing the story. It can be cathartic and provide a means to defuse grief waves. However, repeated discussion may make the person feel drained. Anxiety—or even anger—may then undermine any of the therapeutic benefits the mourner realized from talking.

I recently attended a meeting where a grieving man was talking about a newer family trauma he had been dealing with. As he tried to speak about his pain, his speech patterns were sometimes stilted and hesitant which caused him to be slow in completing sentences. Trying to help, a woman in the group began finishing his sentences for him. Although it was apparent she was just feeling bad for him, her well—meaning help prevented him from being able to expel his own grief at that moment.

After our son died, my husband told me he got so tired of having to talk about what had happened that he wished he could record it. Then every time someone asked him questions, he would just hit the play button and walk off. He understood that people weren't meaning to cause him harm, but the drain of repeating it over and over again, became too much.

Talking about what happened can be therapeutic but depending on how a person may feel at a given moment, it can also increase pain. Before you ask, think about the person who is hurting, and consider getting the information from someone else who is reliable. You may not get all the details, but at least you will have saved the mourner from having to live the experience again.

If you happen to be present when the hurting person needs to talk, just listen. Don't pry for more information about what happened, or interrupt. If the mourner invites you to join the conversation by asking questions, be careful to stay on topic. Watch the mourner's body language while you speak, and keep your responses appropriate to the questions asked. Be careful not to drone on endlessly about the tragedy, or veer off onto nonrelated topics. Track with the mourner by commenting when appropriate, and remaining silent when not.

Although this is mentioned in another part of this book, because this chapter is about conversation, it is worth stating here. If the discussion veers towards memories, consider sharing some of your own happy recollections. Sometimes hearing the good of someone's life can help bring moments of peace in a bad situation.

Chapter 7

LET ME GIVE YOU
SOME ADVICE

Don't give advice. In situations like grief, that is the best advice. When we see suffering people, we seem to have a penchant for wanting to fix them. However, grief is unique, and unlike some life situations, it generally can't be corrected. This means our advice is not going to create an immediate change. Instead, healing of the heart and emotions has to happen before someone can begin to feel better.

In addition, depending on the type of loss mourners' experience, the length of time they suffer will vary. In some situations, the hurting person may only require a brief time for healing. In others, healing could require a longer period of time. However, in some circumstances a residual of pain may remain for life, as is the case with the death of a child (Lichtenthal et al. 2010). In such circumstance, healthy coping mechanisms are the best some people may get.

As seems to be the case with most emotional upheavals, people tend to come out of the woodwork with personal, "expert" advice on how to get better. You can be sure that a mourner has been bombarded with well-meaning counsel. I used the word bombarded here because that is what it feels like. Most people believe they have the answer, and the mourners need to hear what they have to say. Although some of the advice might be relatively harmless, much of it has the potential to be highly damaging.

People who hurt are vulnerable. They don't always think rationally, so they may be tempted to embrace the advice in order to make the pain stop. Because they are looking for hope, they may cling to any potential lifeline, even if it's unhealthy. We might share things we did to cope in our own parallel life situations (i.e., rape, divorce, death, career loss), but we need to refrain from telling a grieving person what to do to get better. Remember, healing doesn't happen overnight. It is a process.

A man shared a personal story with me about his son, who at one time had been addicted to drugs. Some of the man's friends volunteered advice, telling him not to allow the young man back into his home unless he was sober. Those friends had had no training or healthy knowledge of successfully navigating the tough—love model. They just felt that, because they were closely connected to him, they had the right to give counsel. Desperate to help his son, the man trusted them and followed their advice.

The next time his son came home was a snowy night. He was high on street drugs, unfocused, and didn't know where else to go, so he asked his dad for help. Following the advice of his friends, he turned his son away. He said that pushing the front door shut was one of the hardest things he had ever done.

A few minutes later, the man finally looked outside. By the light of a street lamp, he saw his son passed out on a pile of snow in the front yard. He had no coat, gloves, or anything else warm to protect him and was, therefore, susceptible to the freezing temperatures. Seeing his boy in this condition, the man broke. In spite of what his friends had told him to do, he went outside, helped his son up, brought him into the house, and took care of him until he was able to care for himself again. Shortly after that night, the young man realized the condition he was in and got help. I had the opportunity to see him several years later and learned that he had cleaned his life up. He was married and had a child, and was working in a job he planned to make a life career.

Another example involves a man who came home from work one day, to find a letter detailing his wife's desire for a divorce. He was blindsided. He had no idea that anything had been wrong in his marriage, so he was devastated. His wife finally admitted to being unfaithful but agreed to reconciliation. After several months, the wife once again left, saying that she just didn't want to be married to anyone anymore. She wanted to be free to play and couldn't do that as long as she stayed in a relationship. Her parting gift to her husband was to leave him with an STD. The man felt he had given his best to keep the marriage intact, but his wife just wasn't willing, so he gave up trying.

During the course of his grieving process, a friend came to comfort him. At first, his friend operated under the pretext of wanting to provide him support. However, as the evening wore on, the conversation gravitated toward the divorce. At first, the friend offered sympathy and kindness, but eventually the friend's speech drifted away from support to correction. He began making correction statements like, "Next time you'll be more careful about who you marry, won't you?" and "You should have taken more time to get to know her before you married her." However, the man had known his spouse for more than a year before they married, much longer than many do nowadays.

As the friend's diatribe continued, the man felt forced into the unpleasant role of self-defense. He had already been emotionally beat up by his soon-to-be ex-spouse. What little strength he had left, was quickly drained out by his friend.

When the guest finally left, the man called me—broken, shattered, and feeling humiliated by a situation that had not been his choice to begin with. It was bad enough to have to deal with the trauma and embarrassment that generally accompany a divorce. To be further embarrassed and disgraced because of his friend's need to advise him about future relationships was more than he could take.

We all have opinions about how things could be better, and oftentimes, we firmly believe our way is best. But our personal knowledge and opinions do not make us skilled at how to give counsel to someone who is grieving. In spite of what we think, we could be wrong, or at the very least, our advice could be wrong for the person we are trying to help.

Chapter 8

LET SILENCE DO ITS WORK

I n a roomful of people, silence that lasts too long feels difficult and uncomfortable for most of us. Humans, by nature, seem to need communicative interaction of some type, whether they draw it from each other or from the environment at large. That being the case, self—driven compulsory quiet feels unnatural and is unpleasant to embrace.

The temptation to plug silences with speech can become strong, if we feel it is getting too quiet. As is the case with grief, though, our silence might be one of the most important things we can offer someone. In his instructional writings, Solomon stated that there is a time to talk and a time to be quiet (Ecclesiastes 3:7 King James Version). Our silent presence is sometimes what mourners need the most after being battered by a situation and the chaos of comforters who have unknowingly made things worse.

A person drained by pain—and forced to interact with hordes of sympathetic people—, may be left in a state of exhaustion with nothing left to give. Consequently, peaceful silence with quiet support may offer a brief respite from the turmoil. If the person wants to talk, he or she will. If not, though, show compassion and do your best to be a calm presence in the room. Doing this will help the person feel that he or she is not alone or suffocated by speech or touch.

A man whose wife had died found himself inconsolable and in need of help. Hurting badly, he decided to attend church in an attempt to find comfort. Left alone in the sanctuary, he sat asking God for help. As he prayed, a person entered the room, sat next to him, and put his arm around the man's shoulders. The grieving man felt so violated that his prayer changed from, "God, help me" to "God, please make him take his arm off and leave me alone." When the individual finally left, the grieving man once again started asking God for help. After a period of time elapsed, he heard a noise. Turning around, he saw a different person a few pews back, sitting quietly with his head bowed. That person's quiet presence made him feel a measure of comfort, and so his prayer changed from, "God, help me" to "God, please don't let him leave." The man had not wanted to be alone in his grief, but neither did he want to be burdened with what someone else felt he needed.

What we say rarely matters; what matters is what we do. With our unwanted talk, touching, or even staring in pity, we don't want to make the mistake of being a burden on those who are hurting. Doing this just makes things worse for them. Unless we learn the importance and practice of deliberate silence and self-control, we may miss the opportunity to provide *real* comfort to those we care about (Savett 2011). Knowing that we are close by if we're needed may be enough. Being a quiet presence, while letting silence do its healing work in the mourner, is sometimes enough.

Chapter 9

WHAT SHOULD I SAY?

Many people don't really know what to say when something bad happens to someone else. We plan to call or visit, but knowing what to talk about when we do is difficult, at best. We don't want to cause more pain, but neither do we want to feel lost in how to approach the person. Should we talk about what happened? Should we mention mundane things like the weather? Should we try to get grievers to open up to us, or should we force them to listen while we rattle on? Even in situations where we have prepared something in advance, being in the presence of a mourner's pain might actually cause us to lose our grip on our rehearsed speech, and we could fumble around making a mess of what we wanted to share.

Medical and behavioral-science studies conducted about this very topic have shown that words have a significant effect on a person's emotional condition, especially when they are vulnerable (Virtue and Virtue 2010). Speech is a powerful tool that can be used to either facilitate healing or cause further damage. In the Bible, King Solomon wrote that saying the right thing at the right time when someone needs to hear it is a wonderful thing (Proverbs 15:23 New Living Translation). Because of this, we should place high importance on being careful with our words. We want the bereaved to be thankful that we came rather than relieved that we left.

Unfortunately, though, there are no absolute phrases that will guarantee this. What one person might find comfort in hearing, another may reject. This makes navigating the choppy waters of grief a delicate process. Some things we do and say, though, appear to be fairly consistent in helping a mourner. However, before you use any of them, remember that these are not universal phrases that everyone will appreciate. Therefore, use them as a guide and pay attention to their effect on the mourner. If the hurting person grimaces, pulls back, appears emotionless, or does anything else that you interpret as unhappy, avoid using that phrase again. By the same token, be careful not to overuse a phrase.

Never forget that these are only guides. Avoid considering them to be the only statements that will work. You may find a phrase or statement of your own that better fits the circumstances.

The following phrases are divided into three major categories with numerous subcategories. An explanation and example of what a phrase might look like follows each subcategory.

Conversation Behavior

- As a rule, don't clutter the situation with lots of unnecessary speech. We shouldn't force the grieving person to listen to us as we drone on about how bad the situation is, about how we understand, or about things that have no relevance to what the mourner is going through.

There are some instances where dialogue might be appropriate. An example of this might be in the case of bereavement. Sometimes, sharing happy recollections, or positive significant milestones connected to the deceased, can bring moments of peace to a griever. If you are in a situation where this is occurring, consider sharing some of your own—positive— memories.

- Don't stare or send repeated looks of pity. The person's nerve endings probably feel raw, and he or she is most likely doing everything possible to hold it together. Staring, or showing pity does not help them, and it doesn't feel good. It just drives home the point that something bad has happened.

Frequently Accepted Phrases

- Say "I am so sorry" rather than "I'm sorry for *your loss.*" Reminders that mourners have lost something valuable are traumatic. Keeping it brief and simple is the least intrusive way to verbalize your sorrow.

- Say "There are no words." In sharing the story, one person said it was the only phrase people used that didn't worsen the circumstances. This statement allows us to connect with a griever, while acknowledging the seriousness of what the griever is dealing with. In essence, it lets the mourner know that we understand how anything we say will be trite in the face of such circumstances.

- Say "I can't begin to understand." Numerous things contribute to how a person processes pain. Because of this, no one can entirely understand what any person feels when he or she is suffering. A statement like this validates the person's pain and his or her right to it.

- After making a brief acknowledgement, like any of the above suggestions, consider saying nothing else with the exception of that described in bullet one of

Unacceptable phrases

- Don't say "I understand how you feel." This may be the absolute *worst* thing we can say. Even though we may have suffered loss in our own lives, it is highly unlikely that any two situations will be identical. For example, people tend to assume that, just because they have lost a grandparent they love, they fully understand the pain someone is dealing with at the loss of a child. Likewise, being estranged from your spouse does not mean you are going to be able to sympathize with someone who is going through an unwanted divorce. Where this phrase is concerned, it is best not to use it.

- Don't say "It was for the best." When a person hurts, it is rare that the circumstances will be viewed as being for the best. In the case of death, the deceased may no longer be suffering, but the mourner still is. The griever may choose to use the phrase in an attempt to understand why and find comfort. However, we should never repeat this statement back or it could sound placating.

- Don't say "How are you doing?" At a later time, this might be an appropriate question but not at the onset. It should be obvious that someone experiencing loss is not going to be doing well. As such, any answer to this question will highlight the painful circumstances. Understand before you interact with the griever that recent trauma means life upheaval, and the mourner will most likely not be doing well.

- Don't say "At least you know your loved one is heaven." Making a reference to the deceased's relocation to heaven hurts. How can something as innocuous as a reference to heaven be painful? It hurts because it forces mourners to focus on the loss as it relates to the future. Grievers will no longer be able to physically interact or enjoy daily life with the deceased. This means that all their plans, hopes, and dreams involving life with the deceased die also. If hurting people have not yet come to this realization, then bringing it to their attention could cause anger or, at the very least, increase their pain.

Recently, a couple shared with me their story about the loss of their twins who had died at birth. The parents had been anticipating their children and making plans for a future that now would not happen. While trying to make sense of what had just happened to them, a nurse in the room said, "It's better that they died." The nurse's clumsy attempt at comfort effectively drained what little strength the parents had left. Their children—and all the plans the parents had built around their babies—were now gone, and the nurse was telling them that it was for the best? Perhaps the nurse saw the situation that way, but the grieving couple most certainly did not. Sadly, even though time has elapsed since that happened, these parents still remember the pain of the nurse's hurtful words.

About three months after our son died, I received a phone call from a woman I had not seen for several years. I was on autopilot and barely functioning at that time, or I probably wouldn't have answered the phone. The woman asked me how I was doing, rattled on for a few minutes, then abruptly and bluntly stated "You should thank God that your son is dead, because at least he isn't doing drugs like my daughter." Her thoughtless words ripped out my heart. After her call, I collapsed in a chair and cried for a very long time.

The importance of using caution with our words can never be overstated. Although this is especially true in situations involving grief, it is also a good philosophy to embrace for normal interactions as well. When we interact with someone who is grieving, the person is most likely going to remember us for something. We must ask ourselves: Do we want to be remembered as someone the hurting person was glad to get rid of? Or do I want to be someone for whom the mourner was thankful? It is a decision we make based on what we choose to say and do.

Chapter 10

DON'T WEAR OUT
YOUR WELCOME

An important tip to consider: don't overstay your welcome. As discussed in previous chapters, mourners are going to need someone. They are most likely feeling lost and alone. Having someone there when grief waves hit will mean they don't have to suffer without help.

However, sometimes mourners need space to recover. This means solitude to rest. It is impossible for them to feel peace if their home (or life) is cluttered with people. Being alone is not good, but brief moments of respite are important if mourners are to maintain the fragile thread of sanity they are holding on to. This is true at the initial shock of the tragedy, and during its aftermath.

So, how do you know when to leave? The grievers will probably let you know. When you ask them if they need time alone, watch their body language—they might relax and look relieved, or just say yes outright for example. Let mourners know it will not hurt your feelings if they need time alone; if they would like you to stay its ok too. Otherwise, they might feel obligated to let you stay or tell you to leave.

If the person seems indecisive you might consider staying a little longer. Someone who is unsure may not be safe if left alone. In the situation, the individual probably isn't thinking clearly. As such, he or she could be at risk of doing something unhealthy like accidentally overdosing on medication.

Pick up the phone and call. Don't just drop in. It is hard for a mourner to entertain others when he or she is so badly in need of care. Even though your intent is to help, showing up without advance notice may not be perceived as helpful. Consider all the people who have already done this and the toll it has probably taken on the mourner's emotions.

A woman who lost her son said she and her husband had people spontaneously dropping in to check on them for over a year after it happened. At first, knowing so many people cared helped them push through the initial trauma of their pain. However, unrelenting months of unexpected company and forced entertaining wore out the wife. People were coming to her home without warning and staying for hours at a time. Even though the visits their toll on her, the woman didn't feel comfortable asking people to call first. Her husband, who had not dealt well with his own grief, had become numb to what was happening. So the woman felt alone in the circumstances. As the situation continued, her grief grew and forced her to seek additional medical help beyond what she had been receiving.

Being there for someone can make all the difference in the world. Overstaying your welcome, though, can have the opposite effect. People in trauma don't always like to be alone, but neither can they cope with constant people clutter. This is true at the initial stage of grief and in its aftermath. Consequently, when you go to see a mourner, don't leave too early and abandon the person to cope alone. However, don't overstay your welcome either. Consider the individual's condition and match the time you are there to his or her needs.

Chapter 11

SUGGESTIONS FOR HELPING

O ne of the best ways you can really help someone is to make a list of what you are willing to do. After that, contact someone connected to the individual who can give you clear direction, thereby helping you eliminate items that would be unhelpful. Be careful not to assume a family member or close friend will know. If they have not done their homework they will be just as lost as you are, so they will be unable to give accurate advice.

On your list, only include what you are willing and able to do and what you *will* follow-through in doing. If you make promises you can't keep, you may further hurt someone already in pain.

In addition, plan to be in it for the long haul. During the first month after the incident, sympathizers will probably bombard the griever. Although the number significantly decreases by the second month, there still may be a flow of people, mostly by phone. By the third month, very few except those truly devoted to helping, are regularly checking up on the hurting person. By the sixth month, only those committed for the long haul, and closely connected family members are left. With the exception of the deeply caring few, by the end of the first year, most people expect the griever to get over what happened and move on. If you decide to offer assistance or just check up on the individual, go the distance. Don't quit when everyone does because it's just not convenient for you anymore. Keep helping or checking on the person for his or her sake—not giving up for yours.

There are many ways in which you may be able to help. Here are a few suggestions:

1. Bring food.

- Remember to make portion sizes. If you take enough to feed twenty people and there are only two, you have created more work for them. They will have to make room in their refrigerator for the extra food and then have to throw it out later, if it spoils before they can eat it.

- If they have a family, take extra so that the family will have food they can heat up later. This will help ease the burden of visiting family members who may expect the mourner to prepare meals. It will also help provide meals for children who cannot care for themselves.

- If there is a wake after the funeral for family and friends, bring or send food to that as well. There is rarely enough food at those dinners, so the more they get the better.

- Take them a prepared meal each week for the first month. After everyone stops coming, no one may be there to know whether mourners shop, prepare food, or even eat.

2. Help with the house the first month or two. This is *huge* in the zone of providing comfort for people who are debilitated by traumas. If you are unable to help with the house yourself, consider hiring someone else on your behalf. Most of us know teenagers who are always looking for odd jobs to earn extra cash. Some suggestions,

- Mow the yard.

- Shovel the snow.

- Put ice melt on the walk areas.

- Wash the dishes.

- Do general house cleaning.

- Take care of their pets.

- Wash the laundry.

3. Run errands. Grievers barely have the energy to get up in the mornings, let alone go out and shop or take care of business. Furthermore, if they do go out, they may run into someone else wanting details. As time goes on, this should improve. But during the first couple of months, even just the thought of facing more people will probably exhaust them.

4. Take them a card with money rather than a gift. Flowers and plants are nice to have, but in times of crisis, funds

always seem to run low. This seems to be true regardless of the type of trauma suffered—death, divorce, rape, career loss, —and so on. Be cautious of the type of card you purchase, though, as some messages can easily trigger pain (see chapter 9, What Should I Say).

5. Listen, regardless of how many times you have heard the griever tell the same story. We might get tired of hearing a narrative, but the hurting person may need to process a grief wave by talking. Give him or her opportunity to do this by listening without interrupting.

6. Make a few phone calls to locate information about support groups. The type of group you are looking for should match the type of trauma the person is working through. That way the mourner will be able to connect with others who have experienced similar situations.

7. Encourage the person to start counseling within the first couple of weeks after the trauma occurred. It is never too early to begin the journey from hurting to healing.

8. Ask personally if the griever would like help with something. However, it would probably benefit you to wait at least a couple of weeks after the trauma before doing this. Many people have probably promised assistance that they have no intention of following up on. If you wait, you will be able to genuinely fill the holes that someone else left open.

9. Call and check up on the hurting person at least once a month for the first six months. Wait until after the first month anniversary before you begin. When everyone

else has stopped checking on them after the first month, they will still have you as a true comforting resource.

10. Watch for alarm signals. These may vary depending on each person's resilience and history, so make sure what you are seeing is problematic rather than just a momentary grief wave. Of greatest concern are chronic depression and suicide. For more information on these, see section 2 of this book. Ultimately, if in doubt, get the griever an appointment with a doctor's office and let medical professionals decide.

Cautionary Information

Unless this person is a sibling, parent, or closely connected family member, be extremely cautious about how much time you spend with him or her. This is especially true if you are married or in a relationship. Caring taken too far can create unhealthy dependence which may open the door to boundary issues or even sexual affairs. A griever is vulnerable and as such, is susceptible to feelings that can grow from having regular interactions with those he or she perceives as caring. Depending upon the type of loss, the griever could even view you as a possible candidate to replace what was lost. Like it or not, closeness is a breeding ground for unhealthy connections, so protect your own relationship by maintaining healthy boundaries.

Also, don't allow a griever to become dependent on you. Grief is debilitating. If you help mourners too much, they may stop doing things for themselves. If this happens, the mourners will become crippled, needing your assistance to function. Depending upon the severity of the situation, they may need a lot of help during the first four to six weeks or so. After that, they need to start inching backing into doing things. Otherwise, dependence may become inevitable. At first it may be difficult for them to restart life, but if they don't, they could fall into a state of existing, not living.

Section Two

Navigating
Through Grief

Chapter 12

STAGES OF GRIEF

One of the great pioneers in the psychology of grief was Dr. Elisabeth Kübler-Ross. A Swiss American psychiatrist, Kübler-Ross spent much of her time working with terminally ill and dying people. It was during her tenure in this capacity that she began noticing commonalities within the grieving process (Epstein 1993). Deciding to focus on these similarities, she identified five distinct stages that mourners generally travel through when grieving. Even though these phases appear in a categorical order below, in real time they do not follow a specific pattern. For example, people may cycle through depression before they experience anger or bargaining.

It is possible for someone to cycle through these stages more than once during the course of the grieving process. Furthermore, not everyone progresses through every stage. Some may never accept what has happened to them, some may never experience denial, and some who accept the reality of their situation may never bargain. Regardless of how a person travels through these stages, mourners will most likely experience several phases, and some may experience all.

According to Kübler-Ross, these stages may not be complete (Epstein 1993). Although research has identified these five phases as commonalities in the grieving process, a person's response to trauma is still very subjective. As such, people are going to process through their grief in their own way and at their own pace. The identified stages of grief are

- denial;

- anger;

- bargaining;

- depression;

- acceptance.

Denial. During this phase, the hurting person experiences disbelief about what took place and reject the idea that it actually happened. The word that perhaps best describes this stage is surreality. What occurred doesn't feel real. This stage happens when an individual first learns of the loss. The person enters into a state of shock and incredulity, denying the reality of what occurred. As the individual struggles with accepting the truth of what took place, everything around the individual almost takes on a surreal quality as he or she clings to the hope that somewhere, somehow, someone has just made a mistake. It just isn't true.

Anger. Of all the phases a person passes through, this one is perhaps the most volatile. After the shock of what has happened finally wears off, reality sets in, and depending upon the circumstances surrounding the situation, the individual may experience anger. The griever may lash out at others in an attempt to assign blame. The person doesn't understand how this tragedy could have occurred, so the individual begins looking for someone or something to be responsible. In addition to blaming others, the person may self—blame, saying things like, "If I had just," or the more obvious, "It's my fault."

Although not always, the explosions that occur during this stage can be highly dangerous. Venting the anger allows the person to grieve. Allowing anger to run unchecked, however, increases the risk of targeting as a means of alleviation. Targeting occurs when a hurting person wishes harm on whom, or what, is perceived as being responsible for the painful situation. For example, a scorned woman may consider harming the person her husband left her for, rather than her spouse, even though it was his choice to leave.

Bargaining. This stage can be heartrending to watch. It happens when the mourner starts making promises in an attempt to restore what was taken away. These pledges are offered to whatever entity is perceived as having the authority or ability to restore the situation to its former state. Although mourners often direct these promises toward God, depending on the circumstances, they may also direct them at bosses, doctors, estranged spouses, or others.

Depression. After some time has passed since the initial shock, the person begins reflecting on the magnitude of what he or she has lost, and depression may set in. Although the feeling of being depressed is generally part of the normal grieving process, long-term depression is not. With this, the individual's view of life becomes gloomy, and his or her speech may become littered with statements like, "I don't care anymore," "It just doesn't matter anymore," or after having spent hours alone already, he or she still says, "I just need to be left alone." If you are part of the mourner's support group and are unsure if the melancholy is normal or clinical, get the griever to a primary care physician or mental health professional immediately. A person who stays in this condition too long may begin considering suicide as a way to end the pain. More about this is found in the chapters titled "Signs of Clinical Depression" and "Signs of Suicidal Ideation."

Acceptance. The final phase of the process is acceptance. At this stage, mourners begin to accept and deal with the reality of what happened. They understand that it most likely can't be reversed, so they move toward learning to adjust and heal. Acceptance does not mean a griever will always become "normal" once more, though. Just because mourners have begun moving forward with life again does not mean they will be wholly restored to the people they were before the trauma occurred. In fact, the opposite may end up being true.

Severe trauma changes people. Their outlook on life tends to change, as does their approach to daily living and interacting with others. If their journey through their struggles has been successful, they will have found a way to cope, grow, and heal. They will most likely return to doing things they enjoy, and reestablish healthy relationships. They will probably be making plans for the future and, for the most part, once again find contentment in daily life.

As stated before, there is a chance the person may not be the same as he or she was before the tragedy occurred, and we may not like who the healed mourner has become. We were used to the old person and want him or her back. However, because the individual has undergone a major upheaval in life, he or she is going to be different, most likely stronger—and has probably gained healthy, new insights to successfully move forward with life. So, rather than being unhappy about the person we may have lost, we need to support who this person is now. Remember, in a bad situation, the individual survived. Many don't.

Chapter 13

FACTORS THAT CAN INFLUENCE GRIEF

G rief is a very individualized emotional process, and its progress depends on several factors. Although the following is not an exhaustive list, it does contain a few examples of what these factors might look like. At some level, each of these will generally contribute something toward how a person processes pain:

- resilience level
- spirituality or lack thereof
- emotional condition at the moment trauma hits
- relationship position to the loss
- knowledge of impending loss
- support team

Resilience

Resilience—how quickly people are able to recover—is one of the most important factors that determine how they recover. Two individuals may suffer similar losses, but one person might rapidly recover—or, at the very least, handle it better—while the trauma might unbalance the second.

Researchers have committed much time and energy to the exploration of this phenomenon. What might cause one individual to collapse where another forges ahead is a topic of great interest in behavioral science. Although studies are still ongoing, recent investigations have identified the possibility that genetic factors may be involved (Murdock 2010). In other words, some people may just be wired with more strength than others. However, even if resilience is absent in their DNA, people are still capable of learning this skill (Murdock, 2010). As people overcome difficult life challenges, they are tempered and become more resilient. The more hardships people endure and survive, the greater their resilience potential becomes. Likewise, people who suffer few challenges, setbacks, and disappointments may not develop good coping skills, thereby inhibiting the growth of resilience.

Spirituality

The search to find meaning in loss is an essential component of being able to adjust. In fact, scientists have found this element to be positively correlated with an individual's coping ability (Andrews and Marotta 2005). A research study focusing on bereaved parents showed that people who identified with some type of spiritual base were able to ascribe a purpose to their loss, thereby finding survival strength. According to the study, those surveyed stated that their faith had played a key role in providing meaning for the death of their child. Conversely, individuals who failed in their quest to gain understanding increased their risk of poor emotional adjustment considerably (Lichtenthal et al. 2010).

Emotional Condition

As grief is an overarching emotion, the mental state of an individual at the moment trauma hits can have a significant impact on recovery. Obviously a holistically strong person stands a better chance of bearing up under the onslaught of pain than someone in a weakened condition does. Adding strain to an already cognitively taxed individual could result in total meltdown, causing mental and emotional collapse. It is similar to the notion that is the last straw that breaks a camel's back. In this case, though, it is the person's physical/mental condition that disintegrates, rendering him or her barely—or unable—to cope.

Relationship Position to the Loss

It should be obvious that people's grief will be proportionate to their relationship to the trauma—producing event. The stronger the connection a person has to the loss, the deeper and longer lasting the grief may be. The stronger the pain, the more intensely the person will mourn. For example, a person who gets fired from a job may grieve the loss of finances and an enjoyable career. The loss of a coworker's pet however, may barely cause a ripple in the person's life. This is because the direct connection to a job is more personal than an association to someone else's pet. As stated before, the strength of the relationship between the griever and the situation is what determines the intensity of an individual's grief.

Advance Knowledge of Impending Loss

Although this is not always the case, in some scenarios advance warning might weaken the impact of grief. Having advance notice of a possible job layoff provides a person with the opportunity to look for new employment before experiencing financial loss. In some instances, though, even advance warning won't be enough to stave off deep grief. The death of a terminally ill person may be expected, but the reality of his or her absence won't be fully felt until after he or she has passed away. The shock factor might be absent, but the loss could still have a deep impact.

Some of the worst pain occurs when someone is blindsided by trauma. No warning means no time to make adjustments, prepare, or say good-bye. The familiar pattern of life is abruptly disturbed, and not for the better. Uncertainty and apprehension replace normalcy, and the person who suffers the loss is suddenly thrust into a tumult of confusion, pain, anxiety, and fear. Depending upon the type of trauma, advance warning that loss is imminent could avoid—or at the very least—, lessen the impact. For some types of grief, however, nothing helps.

Support Team

It can never be emphasized enough how vital the role of a good support team is to someone who is hurting. Individuals who provide for the needs of a hurting person who is unable to care for his or herself make up the teams. It is in large part because of this group that mourners survive their ordeals.

Support teams do not generally consist of the people you might expect. They may contain some family and close friends, acquaintances, or even those unknown to the mourner prior to the loss. An example of this might be a military family sending aid to the family of their son's fallen comrade, even though they have never met.

The people of this group may not even know each other. They may live long—distances from the griever but know how to stay in touch at the right moments. Part of the group might be a neighbor next door who regularly mows the lawn for two or three months, a friend who takes time to clean the mourner's house, or a family member willing to run errands.

The individuals who make up the support team may never be aware of what the others are doing, and they may never meet. They are just a group of people who have unknowingly united for one specific purpose. Separately their roles may not seem like much, but the combined whole accomplishes a great purpose—to help someone emotionally survive. It is in large part due to these people that mourners are able to begin healing, until they finally reach a state of equilibrium once again in their lives.

Chapter 14

SIGNS OF CLINICAL DEPRESSION

There is a difference between feeling depressed and clinical depression. Where most people may experience some form of melancholia off and on throughout their lives, it generally won't last long. Furthermore, it does not usually cause an emotional damage. It might adversely affect someone's day, but as a rule, it is not going to cause drastic alteration of his or her life routine. In other words, this person is still going to get out of bed, get dressed, go to work, and do other activities of daily living

Sadly, this is not the case with clinical depression. People who develop this condition are no longer able to cope with what has happened, so they quit trying. Their normal daily routine changes from one of healthy habits, such as taking regular showers, to one where they cease to care.

People who succumb to this condition are in crisis and need help. They have deteriorated to a point where they can no longer make healthy decisions about their own welfare, and even if they could, they don't have the energy for it. Consequently, unless others intervene, the risk is high that they could either become suicidal or just waste away.

The following is a list of things to watch for that might help identify whether or not someone is in critical condition or heading for it. This list is not conclusive. It is a point of reference to use in considering potential risk. Unless you are a trained professional in the medical/mental health field, you are not qualified to diagnose this condition. Therefore, if you know someone who is regularly exhibiting these behaviors, get him or her to a primary care physician who can diagnose whether or not the condition exists, before it is too late. Symptoms of this condition may include

- difficulty with concentration, details, and decision making;

- fatigue, sluggishness, and significantly decreased energy levels so that even small tasks are tiring;

- insomnia, difficulty maintaining sleep, early-morning wakefulness;

- sleeping too much or a desire to be left alone to stay in bed most of the day;

- irritability and restlessness;

- continual aches, including headaches, cramps, or digestive problems;

- pessimistic and/or hopeless outlook;

- guilt, a feeling of worthlessness, or a sense of helplessness;

- loss of interest in behaviors or hobbies, including sexual activity;

- changes in appetite, such as uncontrollable binge eating or prolonged loss of appetite;

- panic attacks, unrelenting sadness, anxiety, or feelings of emptiness;

- thoughts about suicide, suicidal planning, or suicide attempts (WebMD, 2010).

Please be aware that people suffering with grief do not always descend into clinical depression. Even if an individual exhibits some of these behaviors, it does not necessarily mean he or she is clinically depressed. The person might just be under a lot of stress or have a mild case of acute anxiety/depression. However, if the symptoms persist, encourage the individual to see a doctor or a therapist, or take the person yourself. A professional in the medical or mental health field will be able to determine whether or not there is a problem. It is possible that, in the end, your concern was unfounded. If it wasn't though, then you may save the person's life. It is always better to err on the side of caution and be wrong, than to live with the knowledge that you might have been able to help someone who gave up trying.

Chapter 15

Signs of
Suicidal Ideation

S uicide has become a major problem in the United States. In 2007, research indicated that it was the tenth leading cause of death in America (NIMH 2010), and there seems to be no abatement in the numbers. Instead, the number of individuals who kill themselves each year seems to grow.

According to statistical data, almost one million people attempt suicide every year in the United States, with someone being successful every 13.7 minutes. Of this group, women are three times more likely to make the attempt and men are four times more likely to succeed. In 2010, 38,364 deaths by suicide were reported. Ninety percent of were identified as having treatable psychiatric disorders like depression. Although every age group is vulnerable, more recently, statistics have identified those at highest risk being between the ages of forty and fifty-nine (American Foundation for Suicide Prevention 2010).

People contemplating suicide generally are not looking for a way out of life; they are looking for a way to end their emotional pain. As such, they don't always share their thoughts with others. Consequently, it is important that we understand as many of the danger signs as we can so that we can stop the attempt before it happens. Some of the common signs are

- a previous suicide attempt;

- statements such as "I want to die," "I'm tired of hurting and just want it to end," or "No one would miss me if I died";

- suicidal ideation in creative writing or artwork;

- making final arrangements, such as giving away articles of personal importance or monetary value, writing or changing a will, paying off debts, making references to burial or funeral preferences, or even writing a suicide note;

- collecting information about methods of death, developing plans, and purchasing the items needed to prepare;

- self-injury such as cutting, scratching—, and so on—;

- sudden radical changes in mood or behavior, withdrawal from normal activities, involvement in high-risk activities;

- a sudden dramatic decline in work or academic performance;

- a sudden drive to finish projects left uncompleted at work, school, or home;

- development of physical issues such as eating disturbances, insomnia, excessive sleeping, and chronic headaches or stomachaches;

- new or increasing unhealthy behaviors involving substance abuse (Washington County Mental Health and Addiction Recovery Board 2010).

As stated in the chapter on depression, remember that— this is not an inclusive list. Therefore, you should not assume that people are only suicidal if they exhibit any of the above behaviors. If you are not sure or even feel a little uneasy, it never hurts talk to the individual about getting help. If in doubt, *always* err on the side of caution.

Chapter 16

SIGNS OF PTSD

Long-term trauma caused by grief also has the unfortunate potential of causing post—traumatic stress disorder (PTSD). The helplessness produced by repeated exposure to a negative incident—, whether in real-time or by reliving it in mental imagery—, can cause a person to react in ways that are not only unhealthy but also psychologically damaging. The coping skills that might develop as a result of trying to handle what has happened can be highly dysfunctional and detrimental to normal life functioning. Consequently, the therapeutic help the person can gain from counseling in times of stress should never be understated, because it can head off symptoms of PTSD.

A variety of behaviors can indicate the presence of this disorder. While both men and women may report feeling the same symptoms, some of the conditions may be more pronounced in women than they are in men. In addition, age and the type of trauma also factor into the strength and type of behavior(s) people might display. For example, children might begin wetting the bed, or they might forget how to talk, become clingy, or act out during playtime (National Institute of Mental Health 2012). These are behaviors adults would normally not exhibit.

Three distinct types of PTSD include persistently re-experiencing the event, avoidance of or becoming numb to things associated with the event, or an increase in emotional sensitivity that previously was not native to the individual's normal behavioral patterns (American Psychiatric Association 2000).

1. Re-experiencing the event may include

   • flashbacks;

   • stressful dreams;

   • reliving what happened;

   • distress upon exposure to something associated with or symbolic of the event (American Psychiatric Association 2000).

2. Avoidance may include

   • working to avoid feelings, thoughts, or conversations that might remind the person of what happened;

   • avoiding activities, places, or people that remind him or her of what happened;

   • difficulty recalling important aspects of the situation;

   • lack of interest in participating in activities;

   • feelings of detachment from others;

   • restriction of affective feelings like love;

- limited or shortened expectations of the future (American Psychiatric Association 2000).

3. Hyperarousal may include

- difficulty falling asleep or staying asleep;

- irritability or eruptions of anger;

- inability to concentrate;

- hypervigilance;

- being easily startled (American Psychiatric Association 2000).

It is only natural that someone who has experienced a traumatic event might exhibit some of these behaviors. As a rule, though, they should not last for a long time, nor should they interfere with normal life activities such as social or occupational functioning. It is also important to note that these symptoms may not occur immediately. It could be six months or more before they show up. Therefore, if you suspect the condition may exist, get the individual to a counselor or doctor for diagnosis and help. As stated before, it is always better to be safe than to live with regrets later.

Section Three

ABOUT ME

Chapter 17

MY STORY

During my early childhood and adolescence I was neglected, and physically abused while living with my parents. Watching my dad handle my mother roughly and treat us poorly was a common occurrence in our home. I believe my mom loved us, but her mental condition was poor. As a result, my siblings and I also suffered trauma by her hands.

When I was young, my mom did not work. That should not have been a problem for our family as my dad made a good wage. He was a very selfish person, though, so little of what he earned supported us. Instead, every Saturday found him dragging us to the local landfill where we would forage for food to eat, clothing, or other items to salvage. When foodstuffs at the landfill were limited, my dad would drive my mom to the blood bank where she gave blood for money; we also went to commodity stations where my mom stood in line for free food. In spite of this, I can still remember times of being hungry.

At the age of ten, I was relocated to my grandmother's house. While in her care, I suffered emotional abuse, physical abuse, and sexual assault. Two of my sisters had already been living there prior to my arrival; my older sister was moved there at the age of two, my baby sister at five. Of the three of us, I was the child she disliked. Because of this, she abused me, physically, and emotionally. Her attitude also made me an easy target for sexual assault.

At the age of eighteen I married, expecting things to improve. However, in my mid twenties a mass was found in my body requiring extensive surgery. That created a chemical imbalance the source of which, the doctors had difficulty identifying. The textbook symptomatology for what I was experiencing contained elements of depression. So the doctors decided that must be what was wrong with me. It wasn't. Due to the misdiagnosis, I developed serious mental health difficulties that took a heavy toll on my family.

Approximately six years later, I was referred to a specialist who taught on the condition originally causing the mass. It only took fifteen minutes for him to identify the problem as a lack of accurate and balanced hormones. Sadly, I had been prescribed the wrong medication, and at a dosage level conducive to a sixty year old woman. By that time, I was in my early thirties. The change I underwent as a result of correct medication was so dramatic, that it prompted my daughter to tell my sister, "I feel like I'm just now getting to know who my mom really is."

None of these life issues, though, came close to what I experienced when our son died. I will never forget that moment as long as I live. Research into grief identifies the loss of a child as being the number one worst ordeal a parent can suffer (American Association of Christian Counselors

2011). Unfortunately, the culmination of my life experiences to date has placed me in the unenviable position of agreeing.

On the evening of July 26, 2005, we got a call a little before seven o'clock. It was the last thing we ever expected to hear. Our older son was dead. He had drowned at youth camp. I had taken a group of teenagers to a week-long camp the day before. Both our sons had gone—one to be a camp helper, the other to be a counselor.

When my husband told me, I dropped to the floor. As I cried, I started denying it could be true. My husband wept along with me. I prayed begging God to let it be a mistake. I willed them to call us back and say, "We are so sorry. It was a mistake. He's still alive." That call never came.

We drove all night to get to the camp. I intermittently cried and prayed all the way there. It didn't help. Five other family members also drove, arriving about one hour ahead of us. Among them were my pregnant daughter and two nieces. When we pulled in a police car was just leaving. I was told that the presbyter called them because he felt my daughter's group was disruptive. They were in *shock*. Appallingly, instead of trying to help them, the police were called.

We were directed to where they had moved the group of teens from our church. When we arrived inside, someone had already assembled them in prayer. I joined the group and prayed for the rest of the night, begging God to bring my baby back to me. While we were praying the bishop and presbyter came in and out several times and stood slightly behind the group. Rather than showing respect for those seeking God, they talked loud enough to be heard above the prayer. They never joined the group.

In the morning, we went to the coroner's office. I prayed the whole way there, seeking God for a miracle that never came. When I finally was allowed to see our son, he looked like he was asleep. But he was so cold. I kissed him and begged him to get up off the table. He never moved. I turned to my husband, grabbed the front of his shirt, and begged him to make our son get up. He just looked at me crying and tried to hold me. I prayed begging God to get our son up. Nothing happened. We were finally made to leave the room.

We went back to the camp. I got out of my car, crying. The presbyter wrapped his hand around the back of my neck and exerted pressure while pushing me toward the cafeteria. I pushed his hand off once, but after a few steps, he put it back and pushed again.

I was lost and, by that time, barely functioning. I couldn't think—I just acted. I went into the cafeteria and sat down. As I did, the bishop came in and sat across from me. Two others sat on either side of me. The bishop kept repeating "I just can't imagine how you feel." I wanted to scream at him, "Do you think that is making me feel better? *Shut up!*"

While I was sitting there trying to talk between bouts of sobbing, someone interrupted to talk to the bishop. Rather than telling her to wait, he just got up and left with her.

Another pastor came and sat in the seat the bishop had vacated. The first thing he said was, "At least you know he's in heaven." I snapped "I don't want him in heaven right now. I want him here with me." I got up and wandered aimlessly around the camp, looking for my husband.

It was sometime before I finally found him. He had been talking to people and looking at the place where our son had drowned, trying to make sense of what had happened. He found out that the area where it had occurred was owned by a private party. It was posted NO TRESPASSING. According to search and rescue, several people a year drown in that spot, so the owners made it off limits by posting the signs. My husband asked the bishop why the kids had even been out there. He was told the former youth director had started taking the kids there several years before. In spite of the signage, no one had ever told them *in person* not to be there, so they continued going.

Two of the camp counselors told my husband that, on that particular day the present youth director, Edward (not his real name), admitted that he had neglected to get a lifeguard. This didn't surprise me as others had been complaining about him for a few years. Once, prior to our son's death, I spoke to the bishop about some of our concerns regarding him. The bishop laughed, and said "He's just twitter-patted because he's getting married." Edward was engaged to the presbyter's daughter. However, the problems had predated his engagement. His serious inability to fulfill the responsibilities of his position is evident in this example. Prior to his appointment, he voluntarily jumped into the same sinkhole where our son would drown saying that he wanted to see what the hole was. It was only because Edward was a strong swimmer that he was able to make it back out. For a few moments, my informant, watching with others at that time, thought they were going to have to call for emergency help.

The counselors further relayed to my husband that Edward had asked one of them to volunteer for the task of lifeguard. No one wanted to. Our son did not know how to swim. This was common knowledge. However, because no one else was willing to fill the role, and our son was the senior counselor that year, Edward *asked* him to cover as lifeguard. Our son should have said no. However, Edward should *never* have asked someone who could not swim to be a lifeguard. As a strong swimmer himself, he was obviously more qualified than someone who couldn't swim. By asking our son to do it he put more than just our son's life at risk. He put in danger the lives of all the teenagers who went swimming that day. A lifeguard, who cannot swim, cannot rescue someone floating toward a sinkhole. They both would have drowned.

Furthermore, when the kids were taken to the river that day, Edward did not secure a lifeguard buddy; provide a life jacket, a life rope, a life ring, or any other lifesaving device for protection. Our son was stationed next to the sinkhole Edward knew was there, and the teenagers were allowed to swim up river from it.

As the story unfolded, we were told the kids were taken in two groups: girls and boys. After the first group finished, our son opted to stay and wait for the next group to arrive. Between groups he was sucked into the hole. The second group noticed that our son was missing. However, per the bishop, the person in charge assumed he was off somewhere so did not search for him. It was not until the second group of teenagers was finished swimming that they decided to look for him. Our son was left in that sinkhole for over two hours.

They brought several people from the camp and began searching for him. Included in this group was my younger son, who had a cast on his arm from a recent surgery. They allowed my younger son to run up and down the river near the sinkhole, helping to look for his brother. Had he slipped, we very likely could have lost both sons that day.

When *they* decided our son was genuinely missing, someone finally called search and rescue. They knew where he was immediately. Going into the sinkhole, they brought him up in a bag. My younger son watched as they lifted him out and then dropped his brother on the ground. No one there protected my younger son from that trauma.

After this story was relayed to me, I got up and went outside still crying. It was then that I learned the reason for the police visit the night before. The presbyter had called law enforcement on my family. According to the bishop, they had gotten out of the van and were loudly searching for Edward, saying they wanted to talk to him about what had happened. The bishop told me Edward hid from them, saying he was scared. The presbyter then called the police.

I was horrified that, after allowing our son to drown, they would add insult to injury and call the police on my family. I asked the presbyter why he would do such a thing. He told me that he called them in case it became necessary to have the girls "taken care of" (his exact words). I later asked the bishop why he would allow the presbyter to do such a thing. I told him that, even in my broken condition, I recognized that the girls were in shock. I didn't understand why didn't they just help them? The bishop became very snide with me and said, "Well, everyone isn't like you, Diane" (his exact words).

The day I had driven the teens to camp, I left the bus keys with our son in case they needed to move it. When we were ready to leave, I told the bishop I was not in a condition to come back and get our church's teens. I asked him to get someone else to drive the bus and bring our group home. The bishop had a commercial driver's license, so he could have done it. Instead, he hesitated, and I had difficulty getting him to commit to helping me. I was standing in front of him crying, looking directly at him, and he still made me ask *twice* before he finally relented and said he would find someone.

They decided to keep camp going for the remainder of the week. I later spoke with one of the counselors. She told me Edward had decided to organize an Airsoft war two days after our son had drowned; he said that he wanted to cheer the kids up. Airsoft is a shooting activity wherein hard plastic BBs are shot out of an air gun at targets. In this case, the kids were shooting at each other. The counselor stated that she went outside and saw teenagers running around shooting each other with the BBs, with no protective gear and no eye covering. She was responsible enough to promptly call a halt to the activity before someone was severely hurt.

Approximately three months later, an ugly rumor started circulating about my family's conduct at camp. My daughter denied it, as did one of my nieces and her husband. Life had spiraled downward for me, I was mentally fractured, and in a lot of emotional pain. But my daughter was very hurt by the vulgar language rumor, so I tracked down its origin. I was shocked to learn that the bishop had spread it. I contacted him to confirm what I'd learned. He admitted that—even though he had not verified the information, he had spread the tale. Because it originated with the presbyter, he just assumed it was true. I then asked why he would spread something like that even if it was true. He was the bishop, after all. He became defensive and short with me, stating that he heard it from the presbyter, and since the district secretary's wife who had been there didn't deny it, he decided it must be true. He never apologized.

I e-mailed the district secretary's wife and the presbyter asking them the same thing. I let them know the bishop had given me their names and that I wanted the rumors stopped. Although the rumors did stop, neither one contacted us to apologize, nor did we receive a response to the e-mails.

One of the worst blows dealt to us by them after our son died, came three months later, in the district's quarterly newsletter. Below is an excerpt from it about the camp. I have purposely chosen not to name the organization involved.

> **CAMPS**
> - In spite of the terrible incident with Nic this year, youth camp was a great success. I was amazed at the way the workers and the teens pulled together and made things happen after the accident. Everyone who was part of that camp, in the most difficult situations, is to be commended for rallying around the kids, the ▮▮▮▮▮▮▮▮▮ Church and the Ashley family. Though there was much mourning, there were also those who kept their focus on the camp and made it happen. The services were

Reading this, my husband and I were horrified—and then angry—about their callousness. To categorize our son's death as a terrible incident, but a mere footnote to the overall success of the camp, was cruel. Furthermore, our definition of being rallied around did not include having the police called on our family, being manhandled by the presbyter, and having hurtful rumors started and spread by officials of the church.

Aftereffects

After his death, I broke down. The first few weeks after the funeral are a blur. Other than our son was dead, I remember very little of that period except bits and pieces, and a lot of pain. I also felt very lost. Even though others were around me, I felt alone.

The day I fully came back to myself was a little over two weeks after the funeral. I was sweeping my kitchen floor, and I remember looking up. My mother-in-law, who had stayed with us during this time, was sitting at the counter watching me. I recall thinking, *When did I get the broom and start sweeping the floor?* As I stood there, my husband passed behind his mom and went out the door. I watched him go and thought *He looks so old.* Looking back at my mother-in-law, I asked her if he had looked like that the whole time. She confirmed that he had and said, "He lost his son and, for a while, he thought he was losing his wife, too." The tears started dripping down my cheeks as she spoke.

As time drug on, every grief wave that hit me caused me to crash. Sometimes I would go into the house, lie on the floor, scream, and then sob into the rug. At other times, I would beat my bed with my fists and scream till I was hoarse. There were also days when I would drive up to our son's grave and lie on it in a fetal position, crying until I made myself sick. I would get back into my car and scream until I was hoarse again. I repeated one of these processes every time a wave hit me.

I spent months and months begging God to please let this be a bad dream. *Let me just wake up and fall on my knees thanking you that my children are all alive and well.* It never happened. I railed at him and asked, "Why, Lord? Parents aren't supposed to bury their children first. It's supposed to be the other way around. The natural order of life is for parents to die first." It felt like my petitions fell on deaf ears.

For about the first eight months after it happened, I would randomly stand and look out the doors in the direction of the graveyard. I kept hoping that if I stood there long enough, he would walk up into my backyard. He never did. All my pleas, all my begging, everything I did never changed anything. Our son did not come back, no matter how deeply I yearned for it to happen.

I was inconsolable. I became suicidal. It wasn't that I wanted to die. I just wanted the pain to stop. Family and friends surrounded us, doing their best to help. But not knowing what to do for people who had lost a child, they felt helpless. With everything that took place, it isn't surprising that I finally became a very bitter person.

Seven months after our son's death, the doctor finally forced me to take anti-depressants. My husband and I started therapy together. Still, it was three and a half years before I actually felt I had begun the process of forgiving and moving forward again. The trigger moment for me was one night during another round of insomnia; I felt God move on me to forgive. I told him how deeply hurt I was, reminded him of everything they had done to us, and told him how I felt he had abandoned us. I felt God acknowledge my pain, but I also still felt he pushed me to forgive. I broke down and started crying hard. I knew that giving up my right to retribution would not absolve them of blame, but it would help make me whole again. So, I made a promise to God in that moment. I promised him that I would forgive, and from that point on, I began to work at the process. I worked to forgive them, and in doing so, I finally found healing.

During all this, my husband also traveled through his own painful journey. He tried hard to hold up as best he could. However, because he is a man and head of the home, people seemed to expect more from him, which added pressure to an already overburdened soul. Eventually, the whole situation took its toll on him, and he snapped. He became short with everyone around him and furiously angry with those who had created the conditions for our son's death. I know he tried his best, but numerous times, I heard him unleash his rage on others for what had happened; he would say it happened because of their stupidity. He intermittently clung to me and then pushed me away, depending on the stage his grief wave was cycling through. He was often rough, harsh, and mean. He had been forced into a highly volatile situation not of his making, and because of it, he became very difficult to live with. Of everyone we knew, only one man in my husband's life had also lost someone close. The man promised to be there for him, but after a couple of months, even he dropped off. So my husband was left to make his way through the morass of his pain alone. When I asked how he felt during that dark time of our lives, he said, "I felt dead inside."

Our family and friends tried to help us, but because more often than not they didn't know what to do, they made things worse. It was never intentional on their part they just didn't know what to do. Without having anyone or anything to guide them through the comfort-giving-process, it became a Herculean, sometimes overwhelming, effort for them. Yet they did the best they knew how.

For us, during that time it was nearly impossible for us to express how we felt. We were dealing with such severe trauma, the mistakes made on top of it all felt like more than we were able to cope with. However, as time went on and we became more balanced, we were finally able to appreciate what everyone did for us.

I have been asked to share what happened to Edward because of his actions, so I will tell briefly what I know. To my knowledge, Edward never received any disciplinary action by the church organization. For their part, the church officials chose to classify my son's death as a "terrible accident", thereby absolving them of responsibility for what happened.

Distraught as I was then, I did contact the district attorney's office approximately three months after our son's death. At that time I was desperate and just wanted justice for my son and my family. The person I spoke with said, had the scenario involved vehicles the circumstances would have been investigated. Because it involved a drowning, though, they looked at it differently. As such, Edward was not prosecuted for his role in what occurred. Although we do not seek out information about him, one of Edward's friends volunteered to us that Edward had continued on in ministry.

Since That Time

My husband and I have talked about how surprised we were that no one from the organization's corporate level ever called with condolences or did anything to try to help us. Although we probably shouldn't have been, we were also astonished that no one involved at the district level ever apologized for their role in our son's death, or for the things that happened afterward.

My husband and I were finally able to forgive those involved. It was the only way we could mentally survive something of that magnitude. We found ways to cope with what happened to us, and in doing so, found as much healing as parents are able to get. It took us several years to reach that place but we got there. This happened because we understood that our healing wasn't about them apologizing; it was about our forgiving them so that we would stop being stuck in the pain of something that can't be changed.

On a personal level, if you are someone struggling with injustices people have perpetrated on you, I encourage you to forgive them for your sake, not theirs. They may never apologize but that does not mean you have to suffer. Healing comes through forgiveness, and with it, freedom.

Conclusion

Personally, I don't think anyone can really be ready to assist someone blindsided by emotional pain. I used to believe my background, occupation, and educational degrees qualified me to understand what a griever needed. However, through my own experience with our son, I have discovered how ill prepared a person can really be when it comes to giving comfort.

There are some basics, if observed, that can help you not make things worse for someone who is grieving though. Also, at the very least, some sacrifices will lighten a mourner's burden, if you are willing to make them.

I wish you success in your journey of helping. It is my greatest hope that, reading this, you will find a way to ease someone else's hurt, thereby helping him or her to heal.

REFERENCES

American Foundation for Suicide Prevention, "About suicide: facts and figures." Last modified 2013. Accessed March, 2013. http://www.afsp.org/index.cfm?page_id=04ea1254-bd31-1fa3-c549d77e6ca6aa37.

American Psychiatric Association, *Diagnostic and statistical manual of mental disorders IV-tr.* Washington, D.C.: American Psychiatric Publishing, Inc, 2000. doi:10.1176/appi.books.9780890423349 (accessed November, 2012).

Andrews, C.R., and S.A. Marotta. "Spirituality and coping among grieving children: A preliminary study." *Counseling and Values.* no. 1 (2005): 38-50. doi: 10.1002/j.2161-007X.2005.tb00039.x (accessed October, 2012).

Carder, D. "After The Affair: Stabilizing Marriages After Disclosure of Infidelity" Recorded December 13 2011. AACC December 13 2011. Web, http://watch.counseltalk.net.

Lichtenthal, W.G., J.M. Currier, R.A. Neimeyer, and N.J. Keesee. "Sense and Significance: A mixed Methods Examination of Meaning Making After the Loss of One's Child." *Journal of Clinical Psychology.* no. 7 (2010): 791-812. doi:10.1002/jclp.20700 (accessed October, 2012).

Lim, W.M. "Revisiting Kubler-Ross's Five Stages of Grief: Some Comments on the Iphone 5." *Journal of Social Sciences.* no. 1 (2013): 11-13. doi:10.3844/jsssp.2013.11.13 (accessed July 12, 2013).

Maraboli, Steve. Goodreads Inc, "Life, the Truth, and Being Free Quotes." Last modified 2013. Accessed July 25, 2013. http://www.goodreads.com/work/quotes/14708444-life-the-truth-and-being-free.

Savett, L.A. "The Sounds of Silence: Exploring Lessons About Silence, Listening, and Presence." *Creative Nursing.* no. 4 (2011): 168-173. http://connection.ebsco-host.com/c/articles/67415419/sounds-silence-exploring-lessons-about-silence-listening-presence (accessed November 2012).

The Biography Channel website, "Elizabeth Kubler-Ross." Last modified 2013. Accessed July, 2013. http://www.biography.com/people/elisabeth-kubler-ross-262762?page=1.

U.S. Department of Health and Human Services, National Institute of Mental Health, "Men and Depression (11-5300)." Last modified 2009. Accessed February, 2013. http://www.nimh.nih.gov/health/publications/post-traumatic-stress-disorder-ptsd/nimh_ptsd_booklet.pdf.

U.S. Department of Health and Human Services. National Institute of Mental Health, "Suicide in the U.S.: Statistics and Prevention (06-4595)." Last modified 2013. Accessed March, 2013. http://www.mentalhealth.gov/health/publications/suicide-in-the-us-statistics-and-revention/index.shtml.

U.S. Department of Health and Human Services, National Institute of Mental Health, "What is Post-Traumatic Stress Disorder, or PTSD?" Last modified 2012. Accessed March, 2013. http://www.nimh.nih.gov/health/publications/post-traumatic-stress-disorder-ptsd/nimh_ptsd_booklet.pdf.

Virtue, D., and G. Virtue. Connexion Pacific Northwest's Journal of Conscious Living, "Choose Your Words Wisely." Last modified 2010. Accessed February 2013. http://newconnexion.net/articles/index.cfm/2010/11/Choose_Your_Words_Wisely.html.

Washington County Mental Health and Addiction Recovery Board, "Learn Signs and Symptoms and What to do if You Suspect Suicide Intent." Last modified 2013. Accessed March, 2013. http://www.wcmhar.org/suicide.html.

WebMD, "Symptoms of Depression." Last modified 2012. Accessed March, 2013. http://www.webmd.com/depression/guide/detecting-depression.

Made in the USA
Charleston, SC
23 September 2013